Sketch

life isn't made for

Perfect People:

Book 1

Topher Kearby

Cover Art by Topher Kearby
Art Copyright © 2021 by Topher Kearby
Cover Design Copyright © 2021 by Topher Kearby
www.TopherKearby.com

Cover Design by Jeremiah Lambert
www.JeremiahLambertArt.com

Edited by Christina Hart
www.SavageHartBookServices.com

ISBN: 978-0-578-88657-2

First Edition
Printed in the United States of America
by Gray Force Publishing

Letter to the Reader:

It's been a long time since I've written a new book. At least it's been a long time for me. I typically put one out every year around March or so, but it's been almost double that time now (a little more or a little less).

I was still writing, though. Still sharing it on my social media pages. Just typing my thoughts out on my typewriters as they came to me. With no real plan to collect any of them in a book or anything like that.

The first part is all new. I was going through some things awhile back. A couple of years ago. Many months ago. Some time ago. It doesn't really matter.

I recorded some of that experience.

I remember not being able to write. I was stuck. And it took everything I had to exist in that space.

I learned a lot. I made a lot of mistakes. I also had a lot of victories. And all of that was good and terrible and everything that life should be.

So, I thought I should write about it.
So, I did.

Now I want to share it with you.

It's a message of hope. A message of purpose.

A message of turning impossible situations into something beautiful.

Life isn't made for perfect people. And I love that it isn't.

I hope you enjoy the journey. Thank you for taking it with me.

-Topher

Life Isn't Made For
Perfect People

Life isn't made for perfect people.
It's made for those
who know how to turn an impossible
situation into something beautiful.
It's made for fighters, dreamers, lovers,
and people who won't give up
even when life feels impossible.

It's not perfect.
It's not easy.

But that's why we're made so damn tough.

Part 1:

The New

Begin

I feel as if I don't know
how to write anymore.
That's the strange part of this book.
I'm working through the idea
that my words have left me,
and maybe they won't come back.
It worries me.

So, I'm just doing it—
writing this book,
and seeing what happens.

Here we go.
Maybe it will be nothing.
Maybe it will be something.
Either way, it will be a journey.

It's time to begin.

Life is a series
of moments
where we are
introduced to
who we will be.

Life As It Comes

The world has been shut down for a while
now, in different ways.
People are discovering parts of themselves
they didn't know were there.
Or parts that were lost.
Tragedies tend to do that—help us focus
on what really matters, and I think what
really matters is understanding
ourselves. The deep-down parts that are
often difficult to process.
They are difficult because they take time.
And who has the time to do that when the
world is spinning as it should?
In a way, that's what happened (for some
people) but I think everyone can benefit
from more time with themselves.
Longer conversations on their own.
Rolling ideas over in their mind like a
child on a sled going down a hill in the
middle of nowhere, experiencing life
as it comes.

Busy

My life is busy,
but life is busy for everyone.
That isn't a reason; it's an excuse.
Being busy is part of the story.
Busy isn't a bad thing.
Not the kind of busy I've been, at least.
I've been *happy busy.*

What then?
What is reaching into my throat and
squeezing my voice so I cannot speak?
Happiness?
Maybe I'm happier? Maybe.

Someone said that to me;
"It's because you're happier."
And I was like, "That makes sense."
But it doesn't really.

Even through my dark days
I've maintained a good amount of joy.
That balance of dark and light
is who I am.

And maybe that's just it;
maybe I've lost my balance.

Rope Walker

The people who step out onto a rope
and walk across the Grand Canyon or
some other crazy kind of location
have always impressed me.
They have such perfect balance,
but they look as if, at any minute,
they could fall to their deaths.

It's wild to watch.
Most make it.
Some don't.

Balance is difficult even for those
who are the very best at it.
I'm not the best at it.
I tend to be kind of terrible at it.

I'm all in and then all out
(usually).
On the rope and then on the ground
(usually).

But, I'm doing better. I'm spending
more time on the rope these days.
One foot after the next,
that long stick in my hands,
my eyes still aching to look down.

Kinesthetic

I put my headphones on in public
so I can block out the noise.
I pull my curtains closed at home
so I can block out the sun.
I press my lips against the bottle
so I can block out the worry.
I lay my head against your chest
so I can block out the pain.

Music is such
a powerful
medication.
It heals
my hidden
sicknesses.

Honest Growth

We write about growth as if
it is a simple thing—
a flower,
a drop of rain,
a sunrise.

But growth is not
a simple thing;
it is war,
it is violence,
it is destruction.

So, let's write honestly,
and live truthfully.

This will be painful.
But it will be worth it."

Happiness

This idea that *happiness*
is always bright smiles
and contentment is a lie.
(I think.)
Happiness feels a lot like
tired eyes and full hearts.
Like dirt under your fingernails
and sweat dripping from your skin.
Happiness is putting your full effort
toward a goal.
Even if that goal doesn't work out.
Even if everything falls apart.

Robe of Words

We wrap ourselves in robes of words—
heavy words,
angry words,
hopeful words,
meaningless words—
because we cannot bare to stand unclothed,
naked and raw,
in front of each other.

What if you don't like what you see?

The scars,
the wounds,
the years of life piled on my chest.

So instead we speak so loudly
that no one will notice the pain.

Even though we should take the time to
look, and understand.

Significant

To be made to feel
significant
as if nothing else
in the world matters
but your happiness,
even for a brief moment,
is the best feeling.

I'm a sunset chaser and a sunrise racer, or maybe I'm just scared to fall asleep.

Humanity

I need to sit and read,
think and dream,
wonder and consider.

I need time with
my humanity.

Most Everything

"That's crazy."

Maybe.

"Then why?"

It's when I feel most.

"Most what?"

Most everything.

I imagine
myself
differently
than I am.

Farmhouse

I bought a white farmhouse
on a little bit of land
just beyond where the sidewalks end.
There are backyard fires
and trees hanging thick with apples.
An old barn sits out back,
and a young cat prowls inside of it.
My girls laugh,
I smile,
and somehow
everything feels right.

Childhood

I remember being small and wild.
I would run through the woods.
I would lie awake in bed.
I would hope.
I would dream.
I would make plans.
I would work toward goals.
I would laugh with my friends.

I would feel insecure.
I would feel out of place.
I would feel as if my brain
were scrambled eggs.

I would manage.

Some things never change.

The more
my sweat mixes
with the dirt
of this earth,
the happier
I am.

Smoke

My grandfather died a long time ago now.
It's been years since I've heard his laugh
or felt his hand against my shoulder.
Time passes and his memories become
more myth than reality, but that's good.
It's good to be remembered as *more*
than end up living as *less*.

I can count the good men I've known
on my fingers.
I've met preachers and teachers
who all ended up being nothing more
than lies and broken promises.

My grandfather.
My father.
A few close friends.
All good men.
I'm lucky in that way.
The closest to me have been the best.

Everyone else promised something
that they weren't.
I carry that truth with me
like embers that won't cool.
They keep burning me
even after all these years.

It's probably why I exhale smoke.

Gone

There is never a good time to
end something good.
Or something that has been good.
Because right at the end, the point
where everything is ready to be over,
you start to remember the "perfect past"
even though those days are long gone.

Gone but not forgotten.

The epitaph on every relationship's
gravestone.

I would rather
end it than
watch it die.

Isolation

I think I'm pushing myself into
an isolation of sorts.
Maybe it is an experiment,
or maybe it is something more.
I've lived a lot. Seen a lot. And maybe
I'm just bored with it all.
I need less. Less noise and less confusion.
A simple beginning and end to the days.

Maybe that's what I need.

Or most likely it's a phase.
Nothing lasts forever.
Life can't last forever.
And so it's better to let
some things run their course.

For now, I'll enjoy the solitude.

Wild

Heartbreakers and
midnight shakers,
those wild souls
that cannot be tamed,
nor would they ever want to be.

They keep the rest
of the world spinning,
with their wild nights
and heads full of clouds.

I worry
that I will
never feel
settled.

Watered Down

I have no desire to be some
watered down version of myself.
A version that is a bit more acceptable
or accessible to everyone else.
I've done that before
and I won't do it again.
These days I'm okay with making people
uncomfortable with my authenticity.
I worry less about what
people think of me,
and I dream more about
the life I want to live.

And I am much happier.

Change

I changed
and you didn't.
Or you grew
and I stayed the same.

Either way
we are different,
and that changes
everything.

There is such
beauty
to be found
in the
quiet moments.

This page is for you. Write your poem here. Whatever you want to write. If you post it on social media, tag me in it and I'll do my best to share it.

Part 2:

Country Songs

Anything Goes

I had an idea for a week or two
that I might be a country singer.
With a pickup truck, an acoustic
guitar, and an old a dog named Sue.
It didn't turn out that way.
(Nothing ever does.)
Because it wasn't who I was.

You can put these words to
whatever rhythm you like.
Pick up a banjo and pluck along.
Maybe a tambourine or a wooden spoon.
It doesn't really matter.
Because these aren't really songs.

Anything goes.

Rivers

We sing about rivers where I come from,
because there's a river
all thick and brown
that flows through the guts
of our small broken town.

It floods the land and covers the roads and
makes nothing more than the farmers'
insurance grow.
This ain't no blue and shimmering stream,
it's an old dirty coward that does whatever
the hell it needs.

We sing about rivers where I come from,
because there's a river
all thick and brown
that flows through the guts
of our small broken town.

In the end, we all drown
and the preacher says it serves us well
because we should have known better
than to build our homes so close to that
brown muddy hell.

Future

I wrote about the future once
with starships and black skies.

I wrote about the future once
with green trees, blue water, and sunlight.

I wrote about the future once
with you and me and a little one.

I wrote about the future once
with you smiling at me while I held our
son.

I wrote about the future once
but now I do my best to forget.

I wrote about the future once
and then it all turned to regret.

I wrote about the future once
but now I'm stuck in the past.

I wrote about the future once
even though I knew it would never last.

Down

I drink the whiskey
down,
down
to the bottom of the bottle.
Down,
down
to the bottom of my sorrow.
Down,
down
until today becomes
tomorrow.
I drink the whiskey
down
to the bottom of the bottle.

And I put it
down
on the counter
and I put your number
down,
down
on the phone and dial
and pray you're not home.
I drink the whiskey
down,
down
because without the burn
I realize I'm all alone.

Bridge Burner

I'm a bridge burner,
always lighting the sky with my pride.
I'm a bridge burner,
I was born with fire in my eyes.

People say, "Hey,
that's not the right way.
You should put down roots
and learn how to stay."

They may be right
but I'll never know,
because when I'm moving I feel alive
and when I'm dying I feel slow.

I'm a bridge burner,
always lighting the sky with my pride.
I'm a bridge burner,
I was born with fire in my eyes.

Some people will judge and say,
"Boy, just stand still."
I'll smile and reply,
"I promise I never will."

This page is for you. Write your song here.
Whatever type of song you'd like to write.
If you post it on social media, tag me in it
and I'll do my best to share it.

Part 3:

The Hits

Proud

I believe that most of us
are doing the best we can
to be the best we can be
in often the most challenging
of circumstances.

That's something to be proud of.

My brain and my
heart speak such
different
languages;
some days that
means I can't
say anything at
all.

Conversations: Part 1

Do you love me?

"Of course I do. you know that."

*I hear your words, but I need
to see it with your actions.*

"What does that even mean?"

*It means I'm tired of being
a ghost in your life. I want
this thing of ours to be real.*

Painful Strength

We both say, "It's over,"
as if we have any control
over our hearts.

You may move on
and I may move on,
but our hearts will never
fully move on.

That's why relationships
can be so painful,
and that's the strength of
real love.

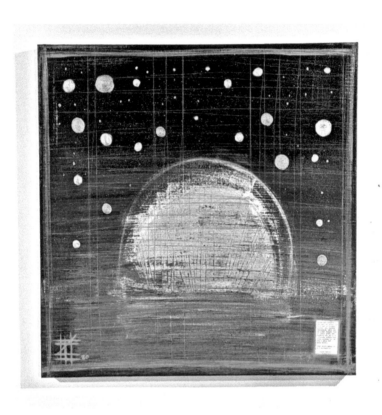

Some nights
I feel like
I am a thousand
broken pieces
scattered across
the sky
like stars.

Heavy

The heart that sits
inside your chest is
just heavier today.

That's why you feel
like moving more
slowly.

Recharge

Why don't you take a break
tonight?

"I can't. Nothing will get
done if I don't do it and—"

And nothing will ever get done again
if you work yourself to death.
Lay down your worries and
come sit with me for a while.

"It's not that easy."

Sometimes we show our greatest
strength when we let our battles
rage on without us for a while,
and give our spirits a chance
to recharge.

Fall in love
with a weird one;
someone not
quite right in
the head.
Life is far more
interesting
when love is odd.

Let's Fall In Love

Let's drink until our
eyes shut tight,
kiss until our lips
quake and tremble,
laugh until our
breaths are empty;

you and I...
let's fall in love.

Time To Heal

I'm working through
some things.
I'm taking my time;
and I'm not going to
apologize for pulling
away for a while.

I hope
because
I still have
breath;
I breathe
because
I still have
hope.

Universe Inside You

There is an entire universe
of *beautiful*
within each of us.
I worry we are
giving it away
too easily these days.

All of who we are is
not meant for everyone.

I Understand You

We all want to be heard,
to be seen,
to have someone say,
"I understand you."

It's simple really;
we all need each other.

I bought her
flowers,
not because
she needed them
but because
I needed
her.

With You

When I'm with you
this world makes sense;
without you I'm a mess.

Right Now

"My past is rough.
I've made a lot of mistakes.
And my future is a mess.
I don't have a plan."

*Your past made you who you
are today, and we will face
the future together. Right now
I'm going to love you just as
you are, and appreciate the time
we get to grow together.*

Difficult Places

You are there
and I am here,
and somehow
those are
the most difficult
places to be
tonight.

I'm Ready

Some see the storms
and say, "This will
be the death of me."

Others see the same
trials and say, "I'm
ready to be reborn."

I feared the
storm so I
became the
storm, and now
the winds and
the waves are
a part of me.

Beautiful Loss

Loss is inevitable, cruel,
and heartbreaking.

But it's also beautiful.

Because it binds us all to one another.
We recognize the struggle and share
our stories about how we made it through.

And that makes us all more beautiful,
and makes life more meaningful.

New

I am made new.

Shedding the past
to make room
for a beautiful future.

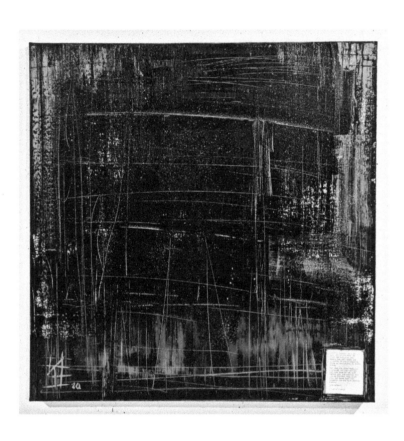

I just need
time with
the universe
tonight.

Don't Rush Your Healing

Sometimes healing looks
a lot like sitting still,
lying down, not speaking,
not moving, and not being
able to process anything
other than the weight of
the universe pressing into
your chest.

Don't rush that time;
those feelings are important.

Fires Of Life

Never underestimate
a love that was forged
in the fires of life;

that kind of love knows
how to fight for what
really matters.

Learning To Trust

Some of us have
been left too
many times to
ever believe that
anything or
anyone will ever
stay.

Hold Me

Hold me tonight
as if you'd lose
everything
if you let me go.

Junk Drawer Human

I fall into the junk drawer of human
existence, in a way that no one knows what
to do with me, or more accurately, I don't
know what to do with myself.

Like some oddball key that
you haven't used in seven years but are
sure it still opens something important,
or a six-foot-long white cable that powers
a device that was left on the beach
three summers ago.

"What the hell is this thing?"

I don't know but don't throw it out.

That's me.
The don't-throw-it-out thing
that's in the drawer filled with other
human beings that don't quite fit
in the silverware organizer or mug
cabinet. And maybe it's a good way to live
and maybe it's also a drag some days
not knowing what you're meant for.

Maybe you're a writer or an artist
or a this or a that kind of person,
and you feel more lost than found.

That's cool.
At least we are in the same drawer.
And maybe that's the purpose of not having
a fixed purpose—

to team up with other misfits and weirdos,
to do amazing things
that have never been done.

A Reminder:

You are stronger
than you think,
more powerful
than you know,
and this world
is lucky to
have your
unique energy.

We're All Okay

There isn't a magic moment when
everything will make sense.
There isn't a morning when you
wake up and feel perfect with every
choice you've ever made.
Life doesn't work that way.
Some days are amazing.
Some nights are impossible.
Some choices push us into
incredible new futures.
And some choices send us crashing
into our painful pasts.

That's all okay.

We're all okay.
Even when we feel the exact opposite.

We're human. We're imperfect.
And that's beautiful.

Dream

It really doesn't
take a whole lot
to keep hope alive.

A little love,
a bit of passion,
and a dream just big enough
to keep you moving toward
a new tomorrow.

You Dreamers

You dreamers,
you wild ones,
you with your hearts
on your sleeves
and hope in
your eyes—
you are the ones
who will truly
change the world.

Never lose your
spark.

Love More, Judge Less

I know my own muddy, messy,
and complicated past.
I understand the mistakes
that I've made.
I remember the wrongs that
I've worked hard to make right.

I also know what I've battled through
and what I've had to overcome
to be where I am now.
It hasn't been easy.
Nothing ever is.
That's why I can't find it in me
to judge anyone else.

Even people who have hurt me or
made choices I don't agree with.
I look at them and I understand that
most of that is because of a past they
didn't choose, and due to circumstances
they wish they could do over again.

I get that.
I'm human too.

I'm going to
love people more
and worry less
about why.

Beautiful Futures

If you spend all your time
judging people for their pasts
then you'll miss out
on the chance to see
their beautiful futures.

A Love That Lasts

We tend to fall in love with
the best parts of people—
happiness, looks, the way they
make us laugh. But real love
stays even we see the worst
of a person. And that's the only
kind of love that lasts.

Weeds

Some of us
are weeds;
we know how
to grow in
the difficult
places.

Alive

I like music that makes
me grit my teeth a little.
like, "Yes! preach. I've
felt that before. Mmm and
that guitar riff moves me,"
and I physically begin to
move—as if leaning into
every powerful note.

I live for that kind of music
because that kind of music
makes me feel alive.

An ocean
between us
and still
we see
each other.

Caring Too Much

"I don't care," I said,
while silently caring
so much that it hurt.

It Feels Right

I write about it because
I've lived it. I've been down. Out.
Scratched off the list. Left for dead.
But I always knew I was still fighting.
Planning. Working hard toward a dream
that kept my fire lit. Now I'm here and
living the life I knew I needed.
Fires and sunsets. Green trees and
a backyard filled with laughter.
Still more to do. Much more.
But for now I'm here.
I'm present.
And it feels right.

As if
I ever
needed
wings
to fly.

Chaos

I am most comfortable
in the chaos.

I am lost when I am
standing still.

The Storms

Yes. The storm did break me.
Scattered my pieces
amongst the sea.
But if it weren't for
those wicked waves
I'd have never found
the real me.

Still Here

"I almost gave up"
isn't a truth you
should be ashamed of.

In fact, you should
be damn proud that
you're still fighting,
still living, still loving,
and still here.

Celebrate that.

Captain

Life is the ocean
and my mind is a river.
Sometimes I drown.
Sometimes I'm found.
Thankfully through it all
I am always me.

Your gentleness
is a gift, your
kind heart is
something this
world needs more
of, and your
willingness to
see the best in
people truly
changes lives.

You Matter To Me

We should tell people
in our lives that we
love them more often.
We should walk right
up to them, wrap our
arms around them, and say,
"I love you, and you
matter to me."

The Human Experience

Seek out new adventures.
Have challenging conversations
with people who see the world
differently than you.
Confront your preconceptions
with new information.

That's the human experience;
we are meant to change.

Authenticity

When I see someone, I tend
to see the best in that person.
I know that's not always the case.
Some people just bring pain.
But I'm okay with that.
I'd rather see the good first.
Even if the bad comes later.
That's why I gravitate toward people
who've made mistakes or
haven't been given the best
shot in life.

Those people are more real.
And authenticity is the
most valuable thing in life.

Love Is Powerful

Speak kindness.
Show love.
Forgive when it's possible.
Put the needs of others before
your own when you can.

Small actions can make a
huge impact on this world.

When you take the time to be considerate,
to be thoughtful, to be truthful,
to be authentic, people see that.
They see your light. And then
maybe they choose to change
for the better.

Love is a powerful truth.

Changing The Thoughts

I want to say that I can do it all.
be everything to everyone,
complete all of the goals
I want to accomplish without missing a
step, and then be happier for it.
This idea is even praised
as some kind of supernatural ability.

But the truth is I can't do it all.
There is only so much time in life.
Add in surprises, responsibilities,
and problems that come out of nowhere,
and then even the time I thought was mine,
disappears.

So, I've changed the way I think.
Or at least I am working to change it.
I no longer see myself as someone
who needs to do it all.
I am someone who is happy doing
what I can with the time I have.

Some days, that will be a lot.
Some days, that will be very little.
But both days I now see
as a success.

I'm Not Done Yet

I'm not done yet.
In fact, I'm just getting started.
I had goals. I had ideas.
I had so many plans for my life.
And they all changed.
Over and over again.
And sometimes that's difficult.
And sometimes that's a challenge.
But most of the time it's a gift.

Because sometimes the place
you really needed to go in
life was somewhere you would
have never planned on your own.

To Ask For Help

It takes a lot of strength
to ask for help. It takes
a lot of courage to say,
"I just can't carry this
on my own anymore."

And it takes a lot of love
to respond with,
"I'm here. You don't have to
fight this alone any longer."

I'm Here

When you take the time to listen,
to understand the situation,
and then do your best to help,
that changes people.
That seemingly small act
can grow into something powerful,
something meaningful,
something that can help remind
everyone that we are all
in this together.

"I'm here to listen."
"I'm here to understand."
"I'm here to help."

Home

Home is the place where
you feel most like yourself.
The real you shines through
with vibrancy and clarity.
Everyone can see and feel it
and you can finally relax.
You can breathe.
You can speak your mind
and have your heart understood.

It's where love lives,
and it can be anywhere
and with anyone,
just as long as it feels like
home.

What's Your Plan?

Tell me about your day.

"I wasn't my best today.
Life took more than it
gave and I failed more
than I won."

So, what's your plan?

"Get up, try again, and
keep going like that
every day until I run
out of days."

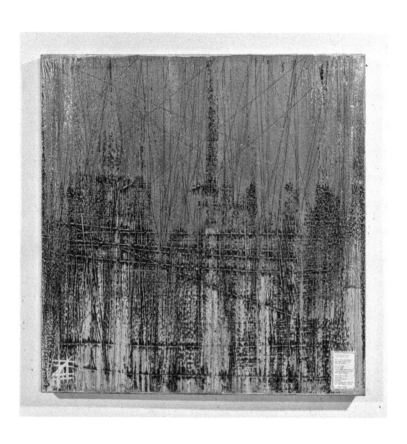

You deserve to be with someone who values your time and understands how lucky they are to have you in their life.

Day & Night

I went the day
without you and
I was fine, but
then the night
came and I nearly
lost my mind.

Grace

Grace, love, and
understanding; they
may not be the cure,
but they sure will
make everything feel
more possible.

Important Question

There is such a
difference between asking,
"What did you do today?"
versus
"What do you want to remember
about today?"

Remember

That's the idea, right?
What do we want to remember?
What do you want to remember? About today.
About the moments you overcame.
The difficulties you fought through.
The time you gave yourself to rest and
heal. The quiet moments. The thoughtful
minutes. The rushed hours. The moving
quickly and the falling slowly.
What stands out? What needs to be
remembered? Not the busy times and the
tasks and the checklists and the
achievements. Not necessarily.
What don't you want to forget?
What do you want to burn into your mind so
next time, you remember? A victory? A
defeat? A conversation that is so
important that to forget it would be a sin?
Hold on to those times. Hold fast to those
memories. Because yes, life is short. But
it's also so very important.

There are songs
that speak to
you, there are
songs that move
you, and there
are songs that
change you—
forever.

Rest & Recover

Tomorrow will come
and it will bring with it
everything it has planned.
My worry tonight
will not change that,
so I will do my best to let it go
and allow my heart and mind
to rest and recover.

Taking Time

Things can be going well.
You can be taking care of
yourself, you can be loved
and be showing love and still
have a day where your
brain hurts and your heart
feels like a bag of broken
glass. That's normal. So,
don't be discouraged.
Tomorrow is a new day,
and we need to give ourselves
more grace and time to just
be.

Beautiful Love

You have a big heart and often
carry the weight of the world
within your chest. It's a gift.
But some days it can feel heavy
and you move a little slower.

That's just as it should be.
People who carry so much love
and share so much love with others
just need time to recharge
and fill their spirits back up.
So don't worry. Now is the time
to give that beautiful love
back to yourself.

Following Your Dreams

If you're exhausted and your body hurts.
If you're emotionally wrecked and your
bank account is drained.
If your friends haven't seen you in weeks
and your family thinks you've lost your
mind.
If the whole world is against you and sleep
is a distant memory.
If your knuckles are white from holding
on and your heart is ready to explode.
If you go to bed with darkness and wake up
before the sun.
If you're used to getting back up after
you've been knocked down—
again and again.

If you're so freaking happy
when anyone else would
be devastated.

You might just be following
your dreams.

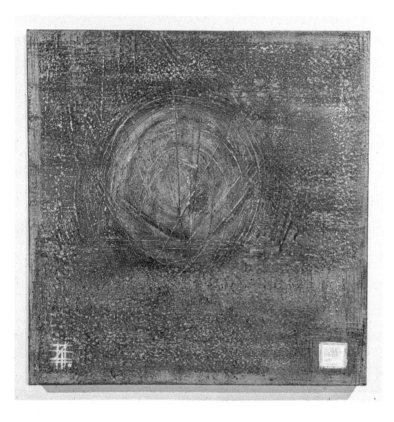

Prove
them
wrong.

Grow.

Chip On My Shoulder

I'm the kind of person who works
better with a chip on my shoulder.
I push harder when I think people are
against me or the system is against me.
That's how I'm designed—
to prove people wrong.
Especially myself.
When I doubt. When I worry.
When I don't think I'm enough.
That's when I know it's time to
step up and prove that I am.
It's time to grow.

Magnificent Mess

Growth hurts more than
you'd think it would. Or
at least in ways that you
didn't expect. Pieces of
you are ripped off and
burned to ash to make way
for the new pieces. There is
fear and worry. And then
there is light. Pure energy
that is born from the ash
and pulses through your
blood and feels as though
it's too much. And it is
too much. That's why who
you were must be laid to
rest. So that who you will
become can be born. It's
a messy business to change.
But that mess is magnificent.

Never Will Again

You are sensitive
and strong,
wild and free,
willing to take risks
and speak your mind.

People call you crazy
because they've never
met anyone like you.

And you know they
never will again.

To Be Heard & Understood

What we feel in our
hearts can often be
so difficult to put
into words, so we
stay silent even though
we ache to be heard
and understood.

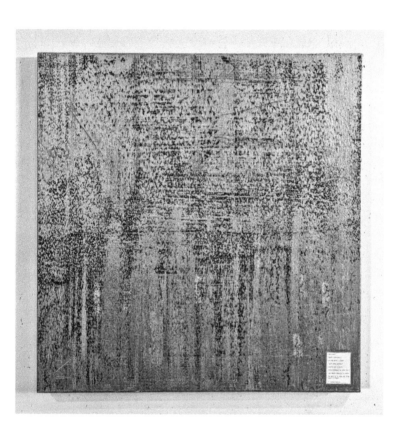

I'm thankful for
the difficult
days I made it
through,
because I now
understand that
those difficult
days don't last
forever.

Difficult Days

I wouldn't choose them if I could. I'd avoid
them at all costs if it were up to me. But
the difficult days have shaped me and
built me into the person I am today. A
person that I'm proud of. A person who is
stronger than I was before. Those days
hurt. They are heavy and at times they feel
impossible. But there is such power in
knowing you can make it through those
days.

And that's what I'm celebrating with these
words.

Truth

It's not, "I understand you, therefore I
love you."
It's, "I love you, even though I do not fully
understand your journey. I want to help
you even though our lives have been
different."

I believe in that kind of truth. And I
believe that it can help shape this world
into a better place.

The Real You

You have to be
a little wild,
a little reckless,
a little weird,
to really make
anything happen
in life.

So embrace it.
Learn to love
the real you.

Incredible Kindness

We all have the incredible
power called *kindness*.

Just a little bit of it can
change someone's life.
A word of encouragement.
An authentic smile.
A few bucks during a rough patch.
A willingness to listen when someone
desperately needs to speak.
It truly doesn't take much; just a
desire to understand that we are all
just people doing the best we can, and
sometimes we all need a bit of help.

Saying
"I love you"
is one thing;
living
"I love you"
is a whole
other story.

Same Words

Just because
we used the
same words
doesn't mean
we said the
same thing.

Kind

"Kind" is the word that's been on my heart
the most these days—thinking about it as
an action. What can I *do* to be kind.
To show kindness. To live with kindness.
Because I believe in that power. The power
we give each other when we are kind to one
another. When we support one another. When
we love one another. And I think that if
more people pursued kindness the world
would begin to heal.

Wander More

Let's wander more.
Let's worry less.

Let's find adventure,
and make plans that
make no sense.

Let's laugh.
Let's love.
Let's keep each other's
spirits high even when
life gets rough.

Let's do it all
together.
From now until
forever.

Let's make the rest of
our days truly count.

Music Is Always The Answer

"What do you want
to do tonight?"

*Let's turn off the lights,
turn up the music, and just
escape it all for a while.*

There is a peace
that can be
found
through
spending time
with nature.

Without You

"I'm not my best today."

Okay. I understand.

"I can't keep a hold on my
thoughts. My brain is on fire.
And it's impossible to focus."

How can I help?

"Just know that today is hard.
If I'm not myself, just give
me some grace."

*Of course. I'm here for you.
I love you.*

"I couldn't do this without you."

*You don't have to. I'm not
going anywhere.*

What now?

"What now?"

Good question.

"Do you have a plan?"

Just keep going.

"That's not a plan."

It's brought me this far.

"And where exactly is that?"

*A hell of a long way from
where I began.*

Love Is

Love is not a gentle
blade of grass, waiting
to be plucked and snapped
in two. Love is strength.
Love is powerful

Love is me
with you.

A Little More Love

It's a good thing to be
someone's happiness. Even
if it's just for a moment.
Making someone feel a bit
better. Or a whole lot better.
Because a few kind words
or a helpful action or a
little guidance can change
everything for someone.

And that's a good thing.
Sharing joy is a good thing.
After all, we could all
use a little more love.

Let's set aside
our worries for
the night and
just love each
other more.

Something Beautiful

There is something beautiful
that happens when we take the time
to see the good in others;

and things really change when
we choose to be the good for
others to see.

Be the love.
Be the hope.
Be the change.

Because people feel that from
you, take it into themselves,
and then give it away again
to someone else.

So, whenever someone asks,
"Well, what can be done?"

My answer will be,
"Be the hope for others
to see."

Take Risks

Love the one
who will dream
with you, who is
up for adventure,
and is willing to
take risks in life.

It's all worth
nothing
if you don't
take the time
to know
the true worth
of yourself.

Your Moment

Bad days happen. Pain can
come out of the blue and
steal the air from your chest.
You fall back and it hurts.
It feels helpless being in that
place. It feels wrong.

But then you stand back up.
You knock the dust off and
set your eyes on the path
before you. You realize that
you're stronger now, wiser now,
and those hard days prepared you
for this perfect moment.

Your moment.

I Change Too

The cooling of the
autumn air.
The vibrance of the
falling leaves.
The brilliance of the
setting sun.
The crispness of a
morning run.

It's all so perfect.
It's all so true.

The seasons change,
and I change too.

The One Who Fights For You

Love the one who doesn't
accept easy answers,
won't allow shallow excuses,
and fights to keep you
honest to the person you
truly are.

Together

Let's just get away
for a while.

We don't need to
know where.
We don't need to
know how.

We just need to know
that wherever we go
and whatever we do
we'll be
together.

Dream
so loudly
that the
universe
has to listen.

I've Been Thinking About This Idea A Lot Lately

You have to manifest it.
You have to make it happen.
You have to put it out into the universe,
over and over again.
If that's what you really want.
If that's what your heart is telling you.
Don't fight it. Embrace it.
Put it in motion. Make the plans.
Take the risks. Let everyone in your
circle know where your passion is
directed. And then do it. It's magical.
It's beautiful. And it's practical.
The more you think about something,
the more you dream about something, the
more you talk to people about something,
the more you write it down, the more likely
it is to happen—because you're making it
happen. That's the real secret. One foot in
front of the other. And before you know it,
you're all the way there.

Manifest

"Aren't you ever worried
about what other people
will think?"

*Never. I'm too busy
manifesting the life
I know I'm meant
to live.*

More Of You

Never apologize for living life to the
fullest.
For squeezing every ounce out
of every day.
For pushing yourself further than you
ever dreamed possible.
For changing your life over and
over again.
For pursuing your passions with reckless
enthusiasm.
For how brightly you shine or for keeping
your head in the clouds.

This world needs more of
your unique vision.
This world needs more of
your vivid light.

All In

People say that you
love too much. Dream
too much. Hope too
much and worry too
little.

But that's okay.
You're all in. You
live each day to
the fullest.

Music Is Happiness

"What's your idea of
happiness?"

Music so good
it makes you close your eyes,
nod your head, and forget
about everything else for
a while.

Who You Are

Who you are does not change
because of a mistake. Because
of a failure. Because of someone's
opinion of you. Who you are
has been built through the fires
and storms of life. Shaped. Molded.
Refined. To live in this exact moment.
Exactly as you are now.

You are powerful.
This moment is valuable.
Don't give it away to fear.

Topher Kearby

I've learned to love the real me; not just the me that everyone else wanted me to be.

Fighting For More

Who I am
is the result of
the trials that tested me,
the pain that broke me,

and the purpose that
kept me fighting
for more.

Brighter

What a gift it is to be someone
who people love to be around. To
be kindness. To be the symbol of
love for others. That's a good thing.
And that's a good heart.

Because life can be hard and
dark and lonely. So, people like
you—people with that light—
make everything feel possible,
and make everything feel brighter.

A cup of tea,
a sky full of
stars, and
enough time
under the
moonlight to
allow dreams
to bloom in
your heart.

These Moments

When things get tough
I've started to tell myself,

"I'm not going to be here
forever. So, what can I
learn from these moments?"

Another Loving Reminder

A few authentic words of
love and kindness can go
a very long way toward
helping someone remember
their strength.

And we all need that
reminder sometimes.

Claim It

There are moments when everything
changes—and you know it. You want
to close your eyes and make it go
back to how it used to be, but you
know in your heart that it won't.
Things are different now. You are
different now. And the world that was...
isn't anymore.

But you won't crumble. You won't
fall to pieces for very long.
Because you're stronger than
these difficult moments and
you're wise enough to know that
a better future is waiting.

You just have to claim it.

We Are All Healing

I've never met a person who
wasn't healing in some way.
We all are. Always. So, take
the time you need to heal.

That time is important.

Life,
please teach me
what I need to
know so I can
let this pain go.

More

The idea that life won't give
you more than you can handle
isn't true. It gives you more than
you can handle as you are now,
and then you have to grow
to make it through

and come out stronger
on the other side.

I'm Not Going Anywhere

"I'm sorry. I know I haven't been
easy lately."

You're too hard on yourself.

"I've been so close to the edge.
It just feels like I've barely been
hanging on."

*And yet here you stand, and
here we are—together.*

"I don't know if I would have
made it through without you."

*That's the thing; you don't
have to. Not anymore. Not ever.
I'm here. Take my hand. I'm not
going anywhere.*

We fell in love
when it made
no sense,
and then
we started
making sense
of the world—
together.

Live Them All

I choose to see the future as beautiful.
As possible. As more than I could ever
imagine. That's the fire in my heart,
and the purpose that moves me forward.

It will be difficult, and I will make
plenty of mistakes. But through it all I
will keep my belief that there is good in
this world, and that there are plenty of
adventures still waiting to be lived.

And I plan to live them all.

Worthwhile

Dream and imagine.
Get excited about the
littlest of things.
Pursue joy. Spread
happiness. Love for
no other reason than
it feels good. Small
moments add up to a
lifetime before you
even realize it. So
don't skip the
good stuff.

That stuff makes it
all worthwhile.

Shine On

There is light in your eyes
and love in your heart. It's
not naivete; it's wisdom.
You've seen the worst the
world has to offer and you've
come out brighter on the other
side. Not because those days
didn't hurt, and not because
people haven't left their scars;
it's because you know that
you're stronger now, and that
strength gives you purpose, and
that purpose allows you to spread
your light to others.

So shine on.
And let love be your strength.

Shape Your Future

Decide who you want to be,
and then become that person.
It's that simple; it's that difficult.
That simple part is the decision,
saying, "I love who I am and I want
to be more." That's a clear path
because that path is forward. It's also
a difficult path, because it will
require everything that you have.

But the good thing is that what
you need is already inside of you.

That heart that beats like thunder.
That mind that burns like fire.

Those are your tools;
use them to shape your future.

Love people as
they are, but
also love them
as they change
and grow.

Many Lives

The idea that we're supposed to stay the
same forever just isn't a reality.
People grow and change and become someone
new. Over and over again. We live many
lifetimes within a lifetime—dying and
being born again into our new selves.
Sometimes it's because of knowledge
learned. Sometimes it's because of
experiences. Sometimes it's because we
simply want to. And that's the beautiful
gift of life. The ability to change. The
ability to start again. And love works like
that too. And to love someone fully, to say
you love people fully, means you are with
them through it all. Through the changes,
through the growth, through the pain and
through the joy. That's love. So let's not
hold someone to who they were or expect
them to never change. Because we all do.
And we all will, all over again. Time and
time again. And that's the only way to
love—fully and completely. That's how I
see the world. And my place in this life.
And it's a beautiful gift.

Follow Your Heart

Whatever you love. Whatever
you are passionate about.
Whatever stirs your heart
and helps your spirit soar.
Go after it. Pursue it.
Learn everything about it.
Make it a top priority in
your life. That fire is
important. Embrace it.

And discover how amazing
life can be when you
follow your heart.

Take Hold

You have to push what's possible.
You have to dream beyond your current
situation. You have to wonder. You have
to plan. You have to make changes that
impact your surroundings.

This is your life. This is your opportunity
to be the person you want to be.

So take those risks,
and take hold of your future.

Mornings Are Magic

Mornings are magic for me.
I wouldn't even call myself
a morning person, but there
is something about a new
day that brings me a lot of
peace and happiness.

I think it's because I carry
so much hope within me and
sometimes it can run low by
the end of a long day. Then the
morning comes and I feel
restored and renewed.

I drink my coffee, step outside,
read a little, clear my mind, and
it begins to feel like anything is
possible once again.

So let me say good morning
to all of you. I know that good
things are still to come.

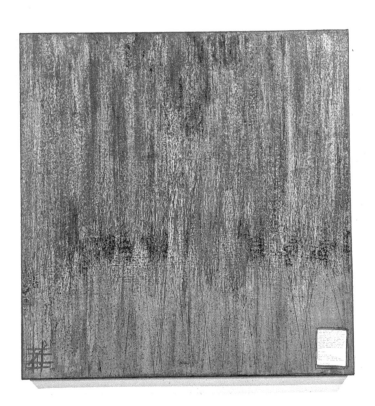

This trial
that you are
currently going
through is
actually a tool
that will help
you grow.

I've Been Reminding Myself Of
This A Lot Lately

Life has been testing me—over and over
again in the same ways. I think I've
learned the lesson. I think I've moved
forward. But the universe still has a bit
more guidance to deliver. So I've gotten a
lot better at listening. Pausing.
Processing the information that I need in
order to grow. It's painful. It's difficult.
It requires long nights and early
mornings some days. And like I've always
said, I'd never ask to go through such
challenges but I'm always thankful I did
when I make it through. So if you're in the
middle of that journey today, know you're
not alone; and that the lessons you're
learning now will make you into a
stronger person for the rest of your life.

Late Bloomer

I love late bloomers. Because I
understand that type of person.
We grew up being chameleons.
We were something to everyone
and it was how we navigated
through life—growing up, high school,
college, or whatever came next.
We were a little of this and a
little of that, for a little of
everyone. It was good, and it
was fine, but it wasn't fully
who we were.

Time goes by, and you realize
that you want to be yourself;
it's that simple and that
complicated.

You ask yourself,
"Who am I? Who do I want to be?"

And then you begin to put your
life together. It takes time—
sometimes a lifetime.

So, if you've just started the journey
of self-discovery, don't give up hope.
You're a late bloomer and the person
you're about to become will be even more
beautiful because of the time you gave
yourself to grow.

Learn To Fix Things

Learn to fix things.
Learn to not throw away
what's good just to get
rid of the parts that are
not working—especially
with relationships, with
love. Starting fresh,
starting again, and
starting over won't heal
your heart. That kind of
growth needs hard work,
understanding, and real
love—authentic love.
The kind of connection
that can weather the
storms and be stronger
for it—together.

Misfit Love

Get weird together.
Get strange.

Laugh so loudly that it
keeps the neighbors up
at night. Make big plans
that seem impossible.
Dream together.
Be different together.

Let your misfit love
shine on.

Real happiness
is when you turn
a situation
that could have
broken you
into one that
helped you grow.

The Power Of Empathy

I've learned to pause when I get
frustrated; to consider the source
of why I'm upset. And it's usually
confusion. My emotions are mixing
with my thoughts and I can't see the
situation clearly. I take a few minutes,
then ask myself, "How can I view this
through a lens of love?"
And once I do that,
I see things differently.

I see solutions instead of obstacles.
I feel kindness instead of anger.
And I see a life that I want to live.

That's the power of empathy.

Fall In Love With Adventure

Fall in love with
adventure, with days
filled with wonder
and surprise.

Life is meant to be
lived with passion.
So let your dreams
grow and your
spirit fly.

Brave Love

Fall in love with a dreamer—
someone who sees the world
as possible and meets new
challenges with hope
and optimism.

Life is far more beautiful
when love is brave.

Real Happiness

It wasn't perfect. It wasn't like
you planned. There were problems
and complications, stressful days
and impossible nights, but through
it all you never gave up. You kept
fighting; and you made it.

Now you're on the other side
of the journey—stronger, wiser,
and ready to meet your future
with a renewed purpose.

And that's what real happiness
feels like.

Twin flame,

I hope I find
you, and I hope
you love me—
in this and
every life
I'll ever live.

For A Little While

Just let me be sad for a minute.
I'll be alright. I promise. But I need to
feel this pain so I can understand it.
Then, once I understand it, I'll begin
to heal. It's part of the process
and I don't need to rush it right now.

So, I appreciate it, I do,
but I don't need advice or
a card that says to smile.

I just need to be sad for a little while.

Myself Today

"I don't feel like myself today"
isn't a defeat. Isn't a weakness.
It's honesty. It's authenticity.
It's saying some days just feel
different. Some moments just
feel harder, or more complicated,
and maybe today was heavier to
carry. Things didn't go right.
Choices went sideways. Or maybe
nothing got done. That's normal;
because the beautiful thing is,
we don't need to feel like
ourselves to still be exactly
who we are meant to be.

So, feel everything. It's all
part of the journey—and it's one
we all travel together.

Hot tea,
long talks,
and evenings
filled with
possibilities.

Tea

There's something about tea
that brings out conversations.
It's the calm.
It's the warmth
radiating from the cup.
It seems to bring out long talks
about nothing and everything.
And always,
in some ways,
feels like love.

Incredible Adventure

Learning to be present is a gift,
because you learn to experience
each moment—the good, the bad,
the everything—and not just skip
over what feels ordinary to get
to what's *next*. Because those
ordinary moments add up to
one incredible adventure.

I may not
understand
exactly what
you're going
through, but I'm
here for you and
will help in any
way I can.

Meaningful Days

Celebrate the things that give you joy.
Surround yourself with people who
encourage you and support your happiness.
Fill your circle with love and hope
for a better tomorrow.

With these choices and this kind of
perspective, you can add so much
meaning and purpose to your days.

In Between Moments

Love someone who sees the beauty
in life, who notices the ordinary
things and takes joy in the
small moments often missed
by others.

Because life doesn't just happen
during the big events; it's found
in all those beautiful moments
in between.

Energy For The New Year

I will be wise enough to
see fresh opportunities,
brave enough to claim
those moments, strong
enough to make the most
of my choices, and loving
enough to support others
on their journey.

Rooting For You

I want you to do well.
I'm rooting for you.
What you are doing is difficult
but not impossible,
and I know the world is grateful
for your passion.

Keep going.
Who knows what this new day
will bring.

Not Alone

Happy people. Kind people.
Loving people. Hopeful people.
Wild people. Quiet people.
Good people. And every other
type of person—can deal
with depression.

So, if you're struggling.
If you don't feel like yourself.
If you're worried about tomorrow
and the night feels impossibly
long.

Know that you are not alone.

You are loved.
And who you are matters.

This You

This you.
This you that you see in the mirror right
now.
With bright eyes.
With dark circles under your eyes.
With frayed hair. With bleached curls.
With pearly whites.
With yellowed molars.
With life painted like a summer sunset on
your face.

This you.
With every bit of beautiful that life has
given you. And every bit of pain.
This you—the you that you are right now—
is a miracle.

Don't forget it.

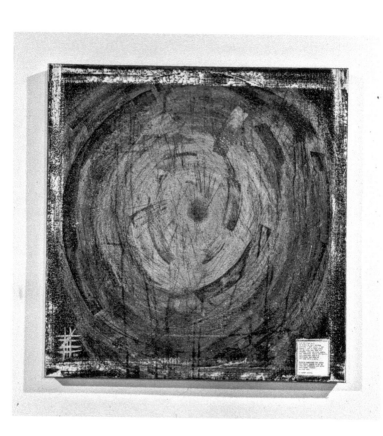

Let's agree to
start again.
Today. As we are.
And not expect
ourselves to be
who we once were
or who we will be
someday.
This moment,
right now,
deserves to be
lived.

Maybe

Maybe tonight is the night
we forgive ourselves.
Maybe tomorrow is the day
we move forward with
our whole hearts.
Maybe this next week is
the week where we find
ourselves again.
And maybe this next year
will be the greatest year
of our lives.

Let's Go

I'm up for it.
I'm here for this.
I'm ready for whatever
is next.
Whatever it takes.
Whatever I need to do.
I'm the one to do it.
My life has brought
me here.
I'm listening.
I'm stronger than
I've ever been.

I'm ready.
Let's go.

Don't Quit

Don't give up. Don't dull your shine just because it makes people uncomfortable.

Who you are is important. What you bring to this world is needed. That fire. That passion. That heart that beats so powerfully inside your chest.

That's the good stuff. That's the stuff people are afraid of. Even within themselves. To let it out. To pursue it. To dream so big it makes the earth shake. That's life. Worry will tell you that you can't do it. Pain will tell you that you shouldn't do it. People will tell you that it can't be done. But your spirit will tell you to keep going.

The more you shed the negative opinions of others, the more you can hear your own beautiful voice speak. And that voice is important. It is on its own frequency.

The words that you speak to yourself are important. Affirmations are real. Speak truth. Speak impossible things into the universe so it takes notice.

Trust me. I've been afraid. I've been terrified. I've been strangled with worry and doubt to the point where I couldn't breathe. But the more I learned to walk in my own shoes and on my own path, the more I

could fill my lungs with the sweet air of a
future that was my own.

It won't be easy. Nothing good is ever easy.
But that's what makes it fun. That's what
makes life exciting. Taking that risk.
Making those tough choices. In your own
way. The kind of ideas that cover your body
with goosebumps and make your hairs stand
on end. Dreams that wake you up in the
middle of the night—not with fear but
with joy.

That's real purpose. When you feel
happiness pulsing through your veins in a
way that makes you feel crazy. At least
crazy in the way the world labels it. But
you're not crazy. You're a dreamer. You see
the world differently. And the world needs
more of you.

So, I'll say it again as I've said it so many
times before: I believe in you. I believe in
your path. Keep fighting. Keep dreaming
and making huge plans that feel
impossible. They aren't impossible.
Nothing is impossible with a driven mind
and a heart filled with love.

I can't wait to see this world shine when
everyone taps into their own light.

Also By Topher Kearby

Watercolor Words

Magnificent Mess

People You May Know

Homemade Mistakes

Contact

Email: TopherKearby@gmail.com
Facebook: @TopherKearby
Instagram: @TopherKearby
Twitter: @TopherKearby

Shop

To order artwork, a custom canvas, or
signed books, please visit Topher's
website(s) at:

www.TopherKearby.com
or
www.etsy.com/shop/TopherKearby

Thank you so much for reading this
collection. If you enjoyed it, please consider
leaving a review.

Lightning Source UK Ltd.
Milton Keynes UK
UKHW020720090621
385189UK00007B/71